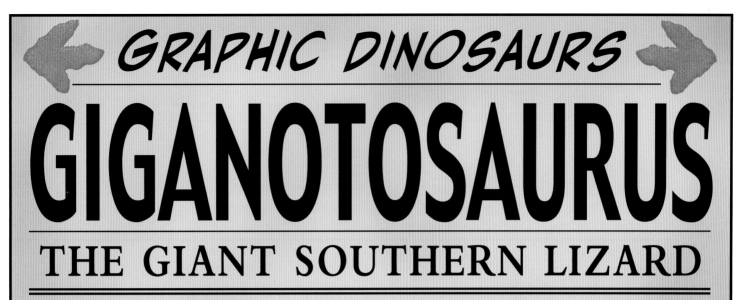

GRAPHIC DINOSAURS

GIGANOTOSAURUS

THE GIANT SOUTHERN LIZARD

ILLUSTRATED BY TERRY RILEY

PowerKiDS
press

New York

Published in 2009 by The Rosen Publishing Group, Inc.
29 East 21st Street, New York, NY 10010

Designed and produced by
David West Books

Designed and written by Rob Shone
Editor: Ronne Randall
Consultant: Steve Parker, Senior Scientific Fellow, Zoological Society of London
Photographic credits: 5t, Jeff Kubina; 5b, istockphoto.com/John Pitcher; 30, Alessandro Abate.

Library of Congress Cataloging-in-Publication Data

Shone, Rob.
Giganotosaurus : the giant southern lizard / Rob Shone. – 1st ed
p. cm. — (Graphic dinosaurs)
Includes index.
ISBN 978-1-4358-2502-4 (library binding)
ISBN 978-1-4042-7712-0 (pbk.)
ISBN 978-1-4042-7716-8 (6 pack)
1. Giganotosaurus—Juvenile literature. I. Title.
QE862.S3S45 2009
668.9'2—dc22

2008003265

Manufactured in China

CONTENTS

WHAT IS A GIGANOTOSAURUS?

GIGANOTOSAURUS MEANS "GIANT SOUTHERN LIZARD"

◄ *It had a good sense of smell to help it sniff out its **prey**.*

◄ *Giganotosaurus teeth were long and flat. Both their front and back edges were wavy, like steak knives. This made it easier to cut through meat.*

► *Its eyes faced sideways. Judging how far away things were would have been hard.*

► *For such a large animal, Giganotosaurus had only a small brain. It was the same size and shape as a banana.*

◄ *Giganotosaurus used its tail to balance its huge head and body over its back legs, like one side of a seesaw.*

► *Giganotosaurus had short arms and three fingers on each hand. It used them to grab hold of its prey.*

◄ *Its heavy body was carried on two strong legs.*

GIGANOTOSAURUS WAS A DINOSAUR THAT LIVED AROUND 95 MILLION TO 90 MILLION YEARS AGO, DURING THE **CRETACEOUS PERIOD**. FOSSILS OF ITS SKELETON HAVE BEEN FOUND IN SOUTH AMERICA.

◄ An adult Giganotosaurus measured up to 43 feet (13 m) long, 12 feet (4 m) high, and weighed 6 tons (5,443 kg).

Giganotosaurus had a 6-foot (2 m) skull filled with 76 teeth, each one 8 inches (20 cm) long.

SHARP TEETH

Giganotosaurus's teeth were flattened and had wavy edges, like a steak knife. The teeth cut into the prey as they bit down and cut again as they pulled back. Giganotosauruses took bite after bite out of a **sauropod** victim. Finally the sauropod would lose so much blood it would die.

AIRHEADS

Giganotosaurus had a very long and narrow head. It was not heavy, though. Holes in its skull meant that it was light but still strong enough to bite its prey.

Giganotosauruses may have lived and hunted in family groups (see page 30), just as African lions do.

Great white shark teeth (left) have wavy edges like Giganotosaurus teeth.

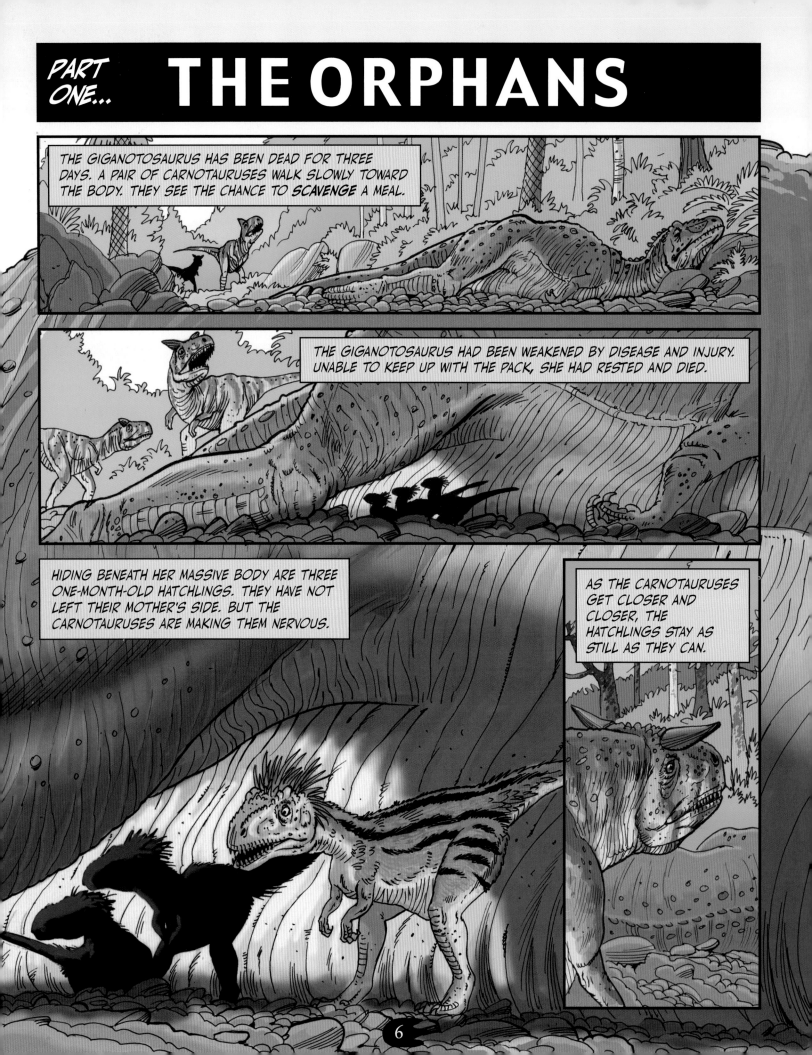

PART ONE... THE ORPHANS

THE GIGANOTOSAURUS HAS BEEN DEAD FOR THREE DAYS. A PAIR OF CARNOTAURUSES WALK SLOWLY TOWARD THE BODY. THEY SEE THE CHANCE TO **SCAVENGE** A MEAL.

THE GIGANOTOSAURUS HAD BEEN WEAKENED BY DISEASE AND INJURY. UNABLE TO KEEP UP WITH THE PACK, SHE HAD RESTED AND DIED.

HIDING BENEATH HER MASSIVE BODY ARE THREE ONE-MONTH-OLD HATCHLINGS. THEY HAVE NOT LEFT THEIR MOTHER'S SIDE. BUT THE CARNOTAURUSES ARE MAKING THEM NERVOUS.

AS THE CARNOTAURUSES GET CLOSER AND CLOSER, THE HATCHLINGS STAY AS STILL AS THEY CAN.

THE UNENLAGIAS CHOOSE ONE OF THE HATCHLINGS TO CHASE.

THEY CAN RUN FASTER THAN THE SMALL GIGANOTOSAURUS.

JUST BEFORE HE IS CAUGHT...

...THE HATCHLING FINDS A HIDING PLACE.

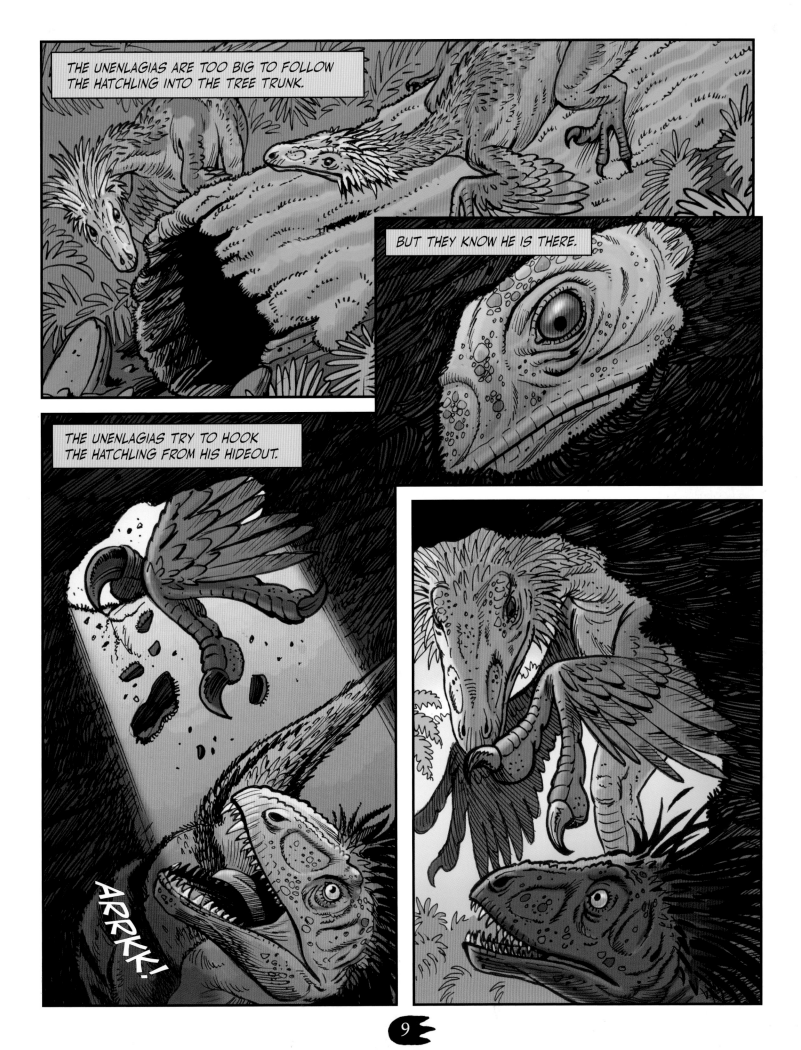

THE UNENLAGIAS ARE TOO BIG TO FOLLOW THE HATCHLING INTO THE TREE TRUNK.

BUT THEY KNOW HE IS THERE.

THE UNENLAGIAS TRY TO HOOK THE HATCHLING FROM HIS HIDEOUT.

ARRKK!

PART TWO... LESSONS

SCARFACE, THE HATCHLING THAT HAD FOUGHT THE UNENLAGIA,
IS NOW TWO YEARS OLD. ONLY ONE OF HIS BROTHERS IS LEFT.

THEY ARE TOO SMALL TO HUNT WITH THE PACK, SO SCARFACE AND
HIS BROTHER PRACTICE THEIR HUNTING SKILLS IN THE FOREST.

THEY PASS A GROUP OF GASPARINISAURAS. THE TINY PLANT EATERS ARE IN NO DANGER.
THE GIGANOTOSAURUSES HAVE PICKED UP THE SCENT OF SOMETHING BIGGER.

THEY HAVE TRACKED DOWN A PAIR OF **JUVENILE** PATAGONYKUSES. THEY WILL TRY TO GET AS CLOSE AS THEY CAN BEFORE AMBUSHING THE INSECT EATERS.

THE PATAGONYKUSES ARE USING THEIR LARGE FRONT CLAWS TO SEARCH FOR BUGS THAT LIVE UNDER THE BARK OF TREES. THEY DO NOT KNOW THAT THE GIGANOTOSAURUSES ARE **STALKING** THEM.

CRACKKK!!

THE PATAGONYKUSES HEAR THE SOUND OF THE TWIG BEING BROKEN. IT HAS MADE THEM JUMPY.

THE PATAGONYKUSES RUN BEFORE THEY CAN BE AMBUSHED. THEY RACE THROUGH THE FOREST WITH THE GIGANOTOSAURUSES FOLLOWING THEM.

ARRKK!!

THE GIGANOTOSAURUSES DO NOT GIVE UP THE CHASE.

ONE OF THE PATAGONYKUSES HIDES BEHIND A LARGE TREE.

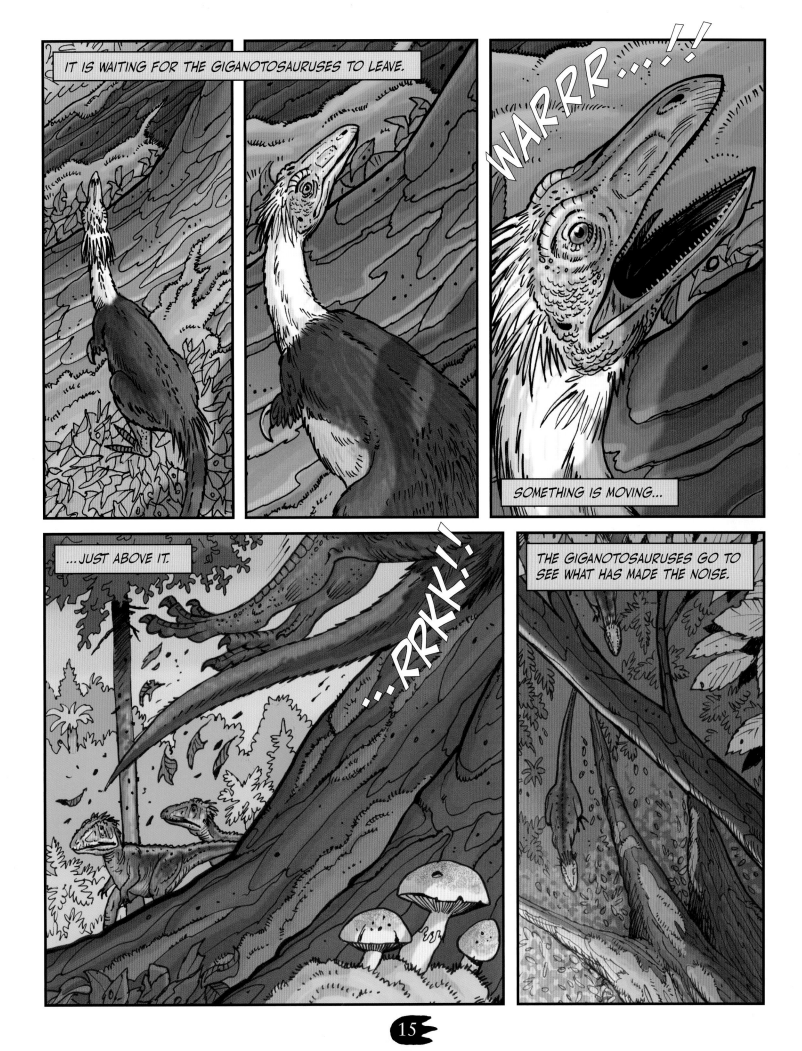

BUT THE SNAKE COILS ITS TAIL AROUND SCARFACE'S BODY

THE SNAKE THROWS ANOTHER COIL AROUND THE GIGANOTOSAURUS. SCARFACE CANNOT MOVE.

SZCHAHHH!!!

BUT THE PATAGONYKUS IS NOT DEAD. IT TRIES TO FREE ITSELF.

ARRK! ARRK!!!

WHILE THE SNAKE IS TRYING TO CONTROL THE STRUGGLING PATAGONYKUS, SCARFACE MANAGES TO ESCAPE FROM ITS GRIP.

THE SNAKE SLIPS OUT OF THE TREE WITH ITS PREY. SCARFACE AND HIS BROTHER ARE NOT BIG ENOUGH TO TAKE THE PATAGONYKUS FROM THE GIANT REPTILE. MAYBE THE GASPARINISAURAS ARE STILL IN THE FOREST. THE HUNGRY DINOSAURS RUSH TO WHERE THEY SAW THEM LAST.

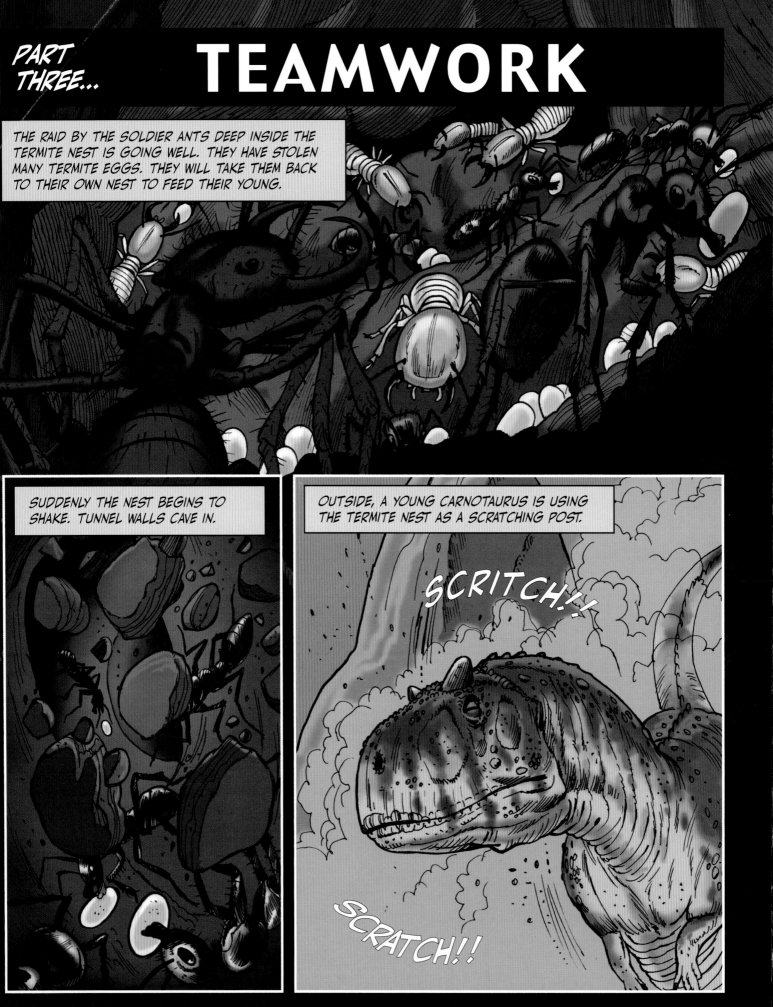

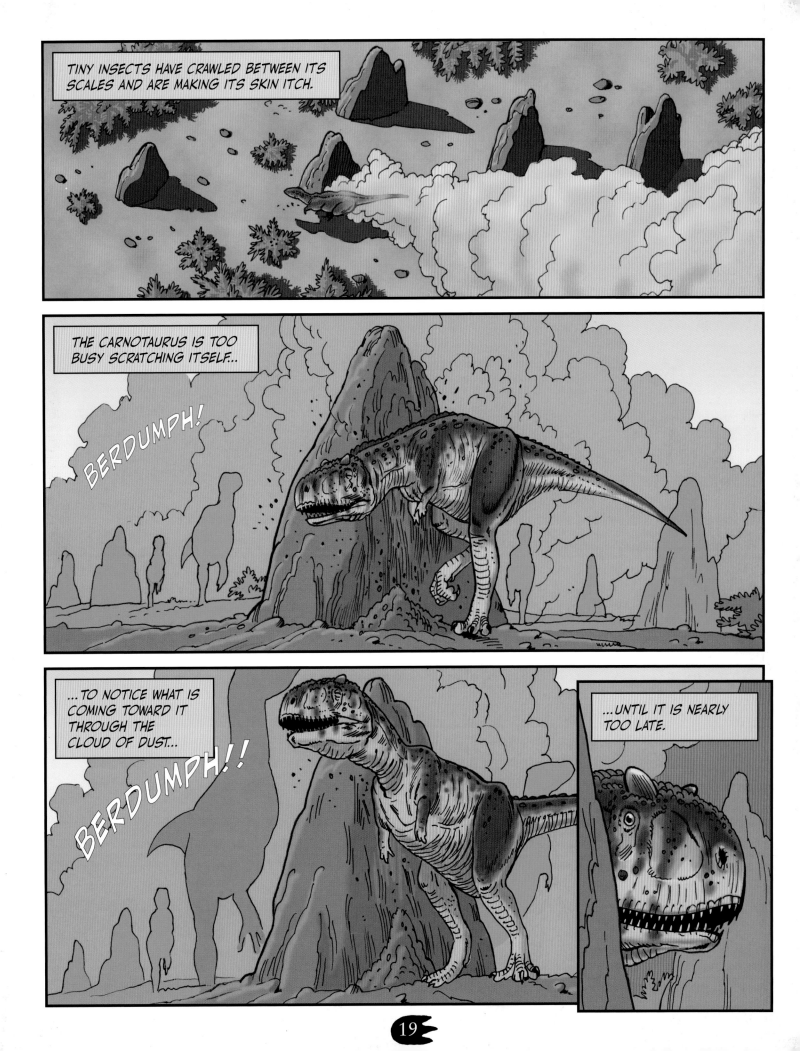

TINY INSECTS HAVE CRAWLED BETWEEN ITS SCALES AND ARE MAKING ITS SKIN ITCH.

THE CARNOTAURUS IS TOO BUSY SCRATCHING ITSELF...

BERDUMPH!

...TO NOTICE WHAT IS COMING TOWARD IT THROUGH THE CLOUD OF DUST...

BERDUMPH!!

...UNTIL IT IS NEARLY TOO LATE.

THE CARNOTAURUS RUNS AS FAST AS IT CAN WHEN IT SEES THE GIGANOTOSAURUSES. BUT THEY ARE NOT INTERESTED IN THE SMALL MEAT EATER. THEY ARE CHASING SOMETHING MUCH LARGER, A HERD OF ARGENTINOSAURUSES.

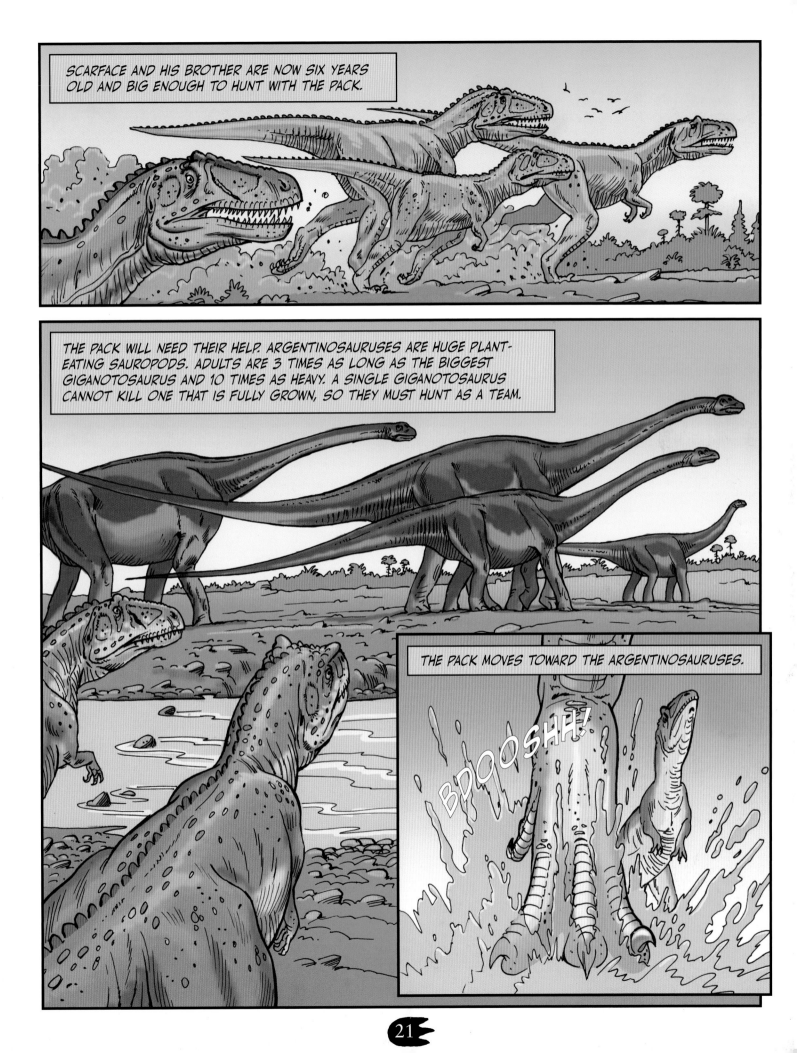

SCARFACE AND HIS BROTHER ARE NOW SIX YEARS OLD AND BIG ENOUGH TO HUNT WITH THE PACK.

THE PACK WILL NEED THEIR HELP. ARGENTINOSAURUSES ARE HUGE PLANT-EATING SAUROPODS. ADULTS ARE 3 TIMES AS LONG AS THE BIGGEST GIGANOTOSAURUS AND 10 TIMES AS HEAVY. A SINGLE GIGANOTOSAURUS CANNOT KILL ONE THAT IS FULLY GROWN, SO THEY MUST HUNT AS A TEAM.

THE PACK MOVES TOWARD THE ARGENTINOSAURUSES.

BDOOSHH!

THE ARGENTINOSAURUS HERD STAYS CLOSE TOGETHER. THE YOUNG ARE EASY TO KILL, BUT THEY ARE IN THE MIDDLE, GUARDED BY THE BIG ADULTS. AND THE ADULTS ARE DANGEROUS TO ATTACK, EVEN FOR A GIGANOTOSAURUS PACK. THEY HAVE SEEN AN OLD AND SICK MEMBER OF THE HERD, THOUGH. THEY WILL TRY TO SEPARATE IT FROM THE OTHERS.

SCARFACE AND HIS BROTHER ARE AT THE FRONT OF THE HERD. THEY ARE TRYING TO GET IT TO RUN QUICKLY SO THAT THE SICK ARGENTINOSAURUS IS LEFT BEHIND.

SCARFACE'S BROTHER DOES NOT SEE THAT THERE IS A HOLE IN HIS PATH.

HE TRIPS AND FALLS...

...BENEATH THE FEET OF THE ARGENTINOSAURUSES.

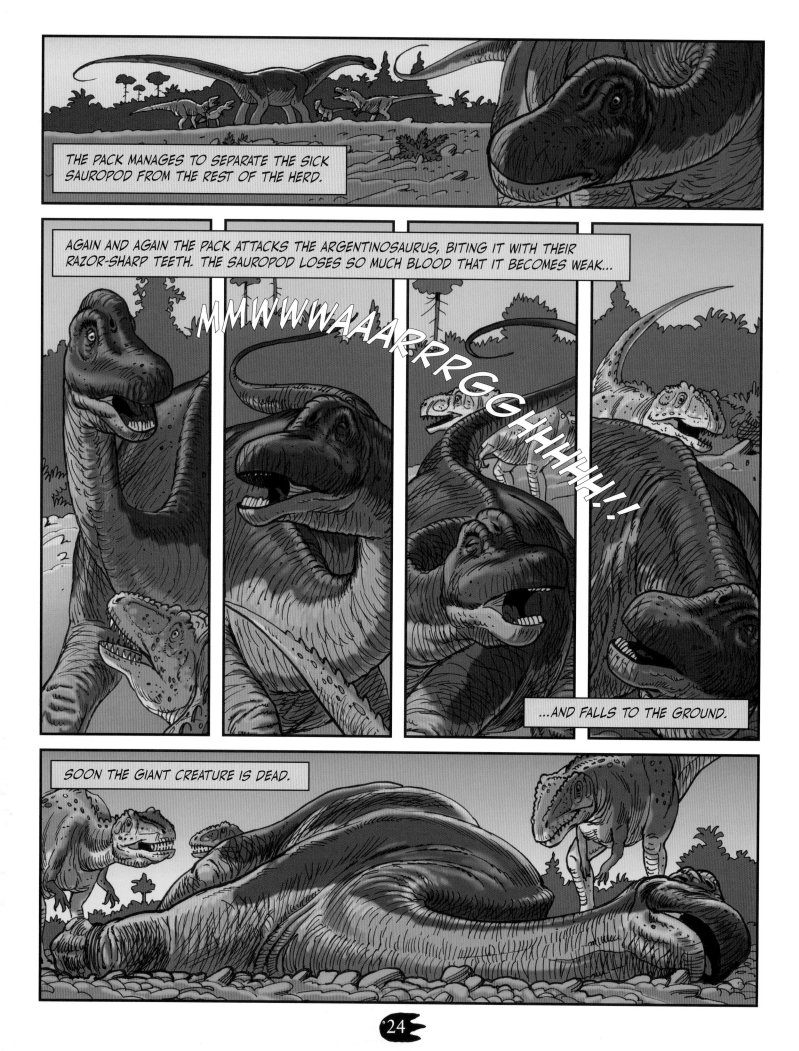

THE PACK MANAGES TO SEPARATE THE SICK SAUROPOD FROM THE REST OF THE HERD.

AGAIN AND AGAIN THE PACK ATTACKS THE ARGENTINOSAURUS, BITING IT WITH THEIR RAZOR-SHARP TEETH. THE SAUROPOD LOSES SO MUCH BLOOD THAT IT BECOMES WEAK...

MMWWWAAARRGGHHHH!!

...AND FALLS TO THE GROUND.

SOON THE GIANT CREATURE IS DEAD.

THE PACK FEEDS GREEDILY ON THE DEAD ANIMAL. SCARFACE IS TOO HUNGRY TO NOTICE HIS BROTHER IS MISSING.

NEARBY, THE YOUNG CARNOTAURUS WATCHES THE GIGANOTOSAURUSES. IT IS HOPING THERE WILL BE SOME FOOD LEFT WHEN THE PACK LEAVES. THAT WILL NOT BE FOR MANY DAYS, THOUGH. IT WILL COME BACK LATER.

MEANWHILE, THE TINY INSECTS ARE MAKING ITS SKIN ITCH AGAIN. IT GOES TO FIND ANOTHER TERMITE NEST TO SCRATCH AGAINST.

AND THE SOLDIER ANTS MARCH BACK TO THEIR NEST CARRYING THEIR TERMITE EGGS.

THE GIGANOTOSAURUSES HAVE KILLED A YOUNG ARGENTINOSAURUS. THE PACK FEEDS ON IT EVEN THOUGH A STORM IS COMING. SCARFACE IS NOW 12 YEARS OLD AND AN ADULT. THE PACK'S LEADER IS A LARGE FEMALE.

THE SMELL OF THE DEAD SAUROPOD HAS DRAWN A SMALL PACK OF MAPUSAURUSES. THEIR LEADER IS A HUGE MALE, BIGGER THAN ANY OF THE GIGANOTOSAURUSES. THEY WANT TO STEAL THE PACK'S KILL. THE BIG MAPUSAURUS ROARS OUT A CHALLENGE TO THE GIGANOTOSAURUSES.

WARRRGHH!!

THE GIGANOTOSAURUS LEADER WILL NOT LET THE MAPUSAURUSES HAVE THE SAUROPOD WITHOUT A FIGHT.

26

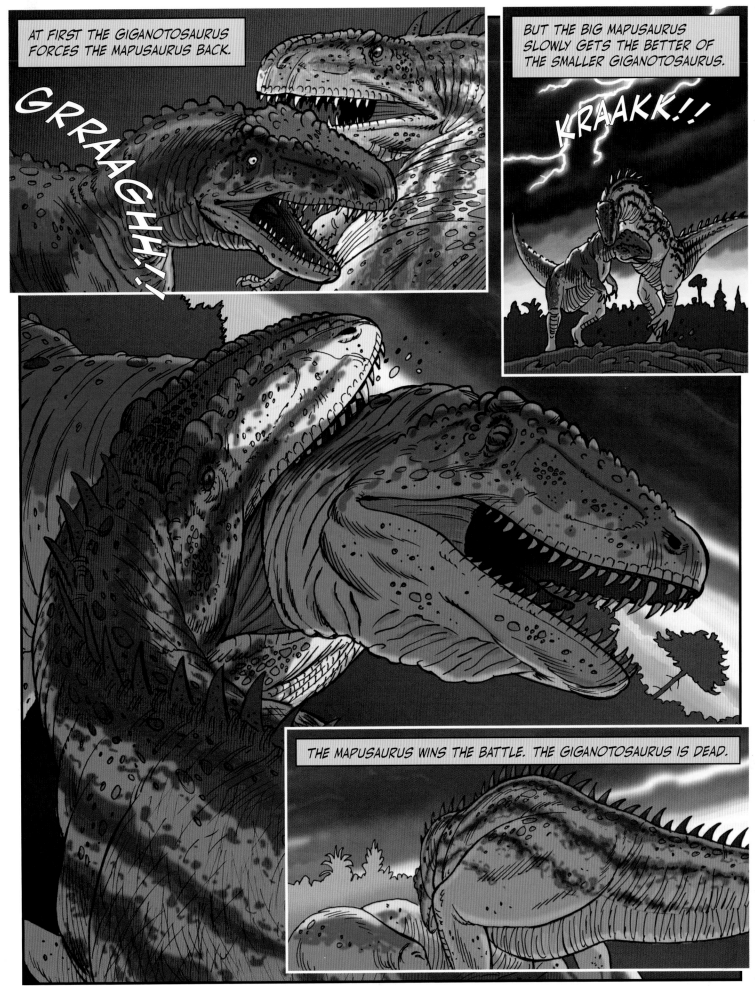

AT FIRST THE GIGANOTOSAURUS FORCES THE MAPUSAURUS BACK.

GRRAAGHH!!

BUT THE BIG MAPUSAURUS SLOWLY GETS THE BETTER OF THE SMALLER GIGANOTOSAURUS.

KRAAKK!!

THE MAPUSAURUS WINS THE BATTLE. THE GIGANOTOSAURUS IS DEAD.

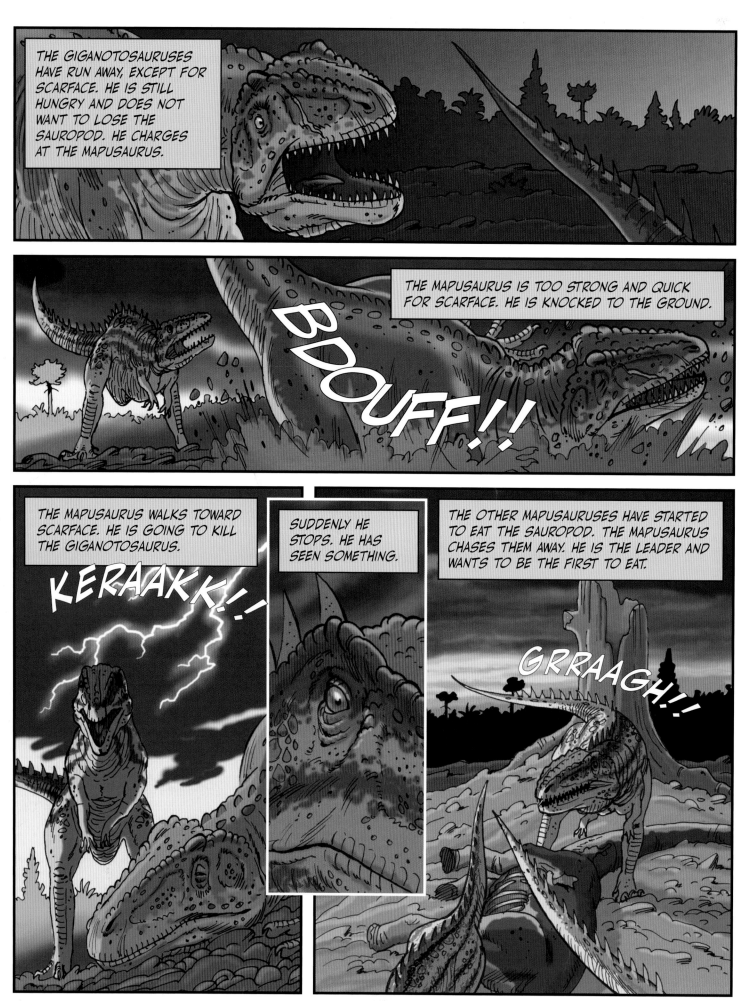

THE GIGANOTOSAURUSES HAVE RUN AWAY, EXCEPT FOR SCARFACE. HE IS STILL HUNGRY AND DOES NOT WANT TO LOSE THE SAUROPOD. HE CHARGES AT THE MAPUSAURUS.

THE MAPUSAURUS IS TOO STRONG AND QUICK FOR SCARFACE. HE IS KNOCKED TO THE GROUND.

BDOUFF!!!

THE MAPUSAURUS WALKS TOWARD SCARFACE. HE IS GOING TO KILL THE GIGANOTOSAURUS.

KERAAKK!!!

SUDDENLY HE STOPS. HE HAS SEEN SOMETHING.

THE OTHER MAPUSAURUSES HAVE STARTED TO EAT THE SAUROPOD. THE MAPUSAURUS CHASES THEM AWAY. HE IS THE LEADER AND WANTS TO BE THE FIRST TO EAT.

GRRAAGH!!!

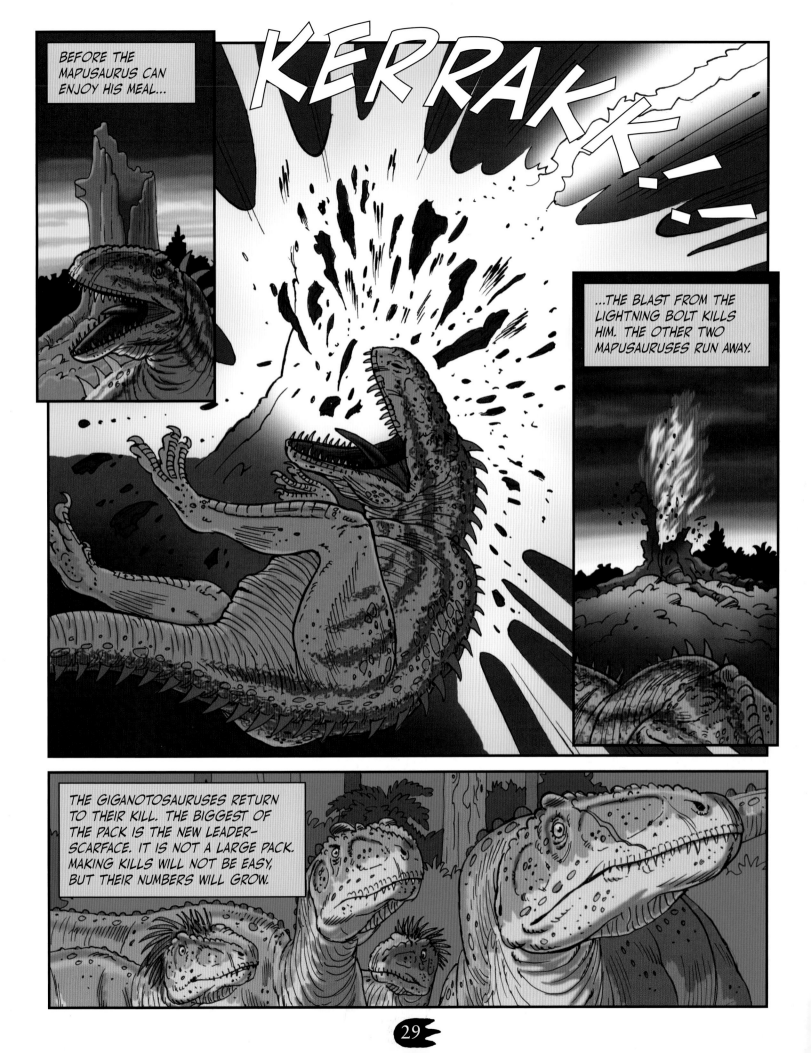

BEFORE THE MAPUSAURUS CAN ENJOY HIS MEAL...

KERRAKK!

...THE BLAST FROM THE LIGHTNING BOLT KILLS HIM. THE OTHER TWO MAPUSAURUSES RUN AWAY.

THE GIGANOTOSAURUSES RETURN TO THEIR KILL. THE BIGGEST OF THE PACK IS THE NEW LEADER-SCARFACE. IT IS NOT A LARGE PACK. MAKING KILLS WILL NOT BE EASY, BUT THEIR NUMBERS WILL GROW.

FOSSIL EVIDENCE

SCIENTISTS LEARN WHAT DINOSAURS MAY HAVE LOOKED LIKE BY STUDYING THEIR FOSSIL REMAINS. FOSSILS ARE FORMED WHEN THE HARD PARTS OF AN ANIMAL OR PLANT BECOME BURIED AND TURN TO ROCK OVER THOUSANDS OF YEARS.

The picture below shows a Giganotosaurus attacking a huge sauropod called an Argentinosaurus. Giganotosaurus was first found in 1993 in Argentina, South America. Near it was the fossilized skeleton of a 75-foot- (23-m) long sauropod. Scientists believe that these large plant-eating dinosaurs were hunted by Giganotosauruses. But the full-grown sauropods were very big.

Could a single Giganotosaurus kill an animal ten times heavier than itself? In 1997 seven fossilized Mapusauruses were found together. They had died at the same time. They may have been a family group, because there were young and old animals. As Mapusauruses were related to Giganotosauruses, both animals could have hunted the big sauropods in packs.

ANIMAL GALLERY

ALL THESE ANIMALS APPEAR IN THE STORY.

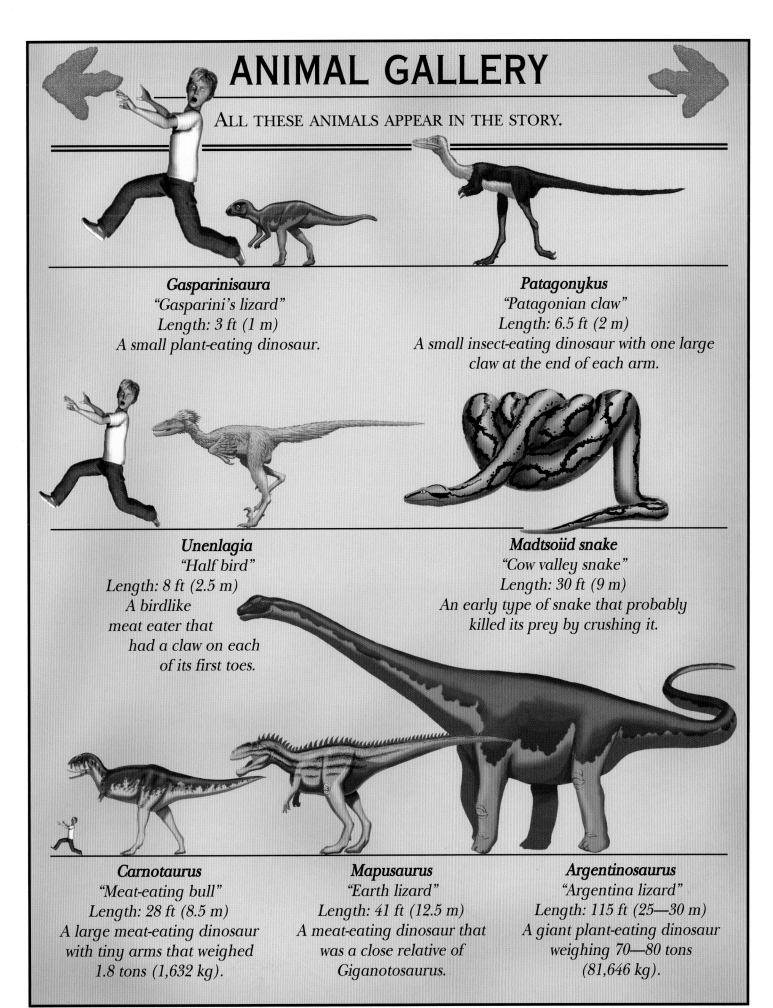

Gasparinisaura
"Gasparini's lizard"
Length: 3 ft (1 m)
A small plant-eating dinosaur.

Patagonykus
"Patagonian claw"
Length: 6.5 ft (2 m)
A small insect-eating dinosaur with one large claw at the end of each arm.

Unenlagia
"Half bird"
Length: 8 ft (2.5 m)
A birdlike meat eater that had a claw on each of its first toes.

Madtsoïid snake
"Cow valley snake"
Length: 30 ft (9 m)
An early type of snake that probably killed its prey by crushing it.

Carnotaurus
"Meat-eating bull"
Length: 28 ft (8.5 m)
A large meat-eating dinosaur with tiny arms that weighed 1.8 tons (1,632 kg).

Mapusaurus
"Earth lizard"
Length: 41 ft (12.5 m)
A meat-eating dinosaur that was a close relative of Giganotosaurus.

Argentinosaurus
"Argentina lizard"
Length: 115 ft (25—30 m)
A giant plant-eating dinosaur weighing 70—80 tons (81,646 kg).

GLOSSARY

ambush (AM-bush) To attack from a hiding place.

Cretaceous period (krih-TAY-shus PIR-ee-ud) The time between 145 million and 65 million years ago.

fossils (FAH-sulz) The remains of living things that have turned to rock.

juvenile (JOO-veh-ny-uhl) A young animal that is not fully grown.

prey (PRAY) Animals that are hunted for food by another animal.

sauropod (SAWR-uh-pod) Any of a group of the largest four-footed, plant-eating dinosaurs with long necks and tails and small heads.

scavenge (SKA-venj) To search for dead animals to eat.

stalking (STAW-king) Secretly following someone.

INDEX

Web Sites
Due to the changing nature of Internet links, the Rosen Publishing Group, Inc., has developed an online list of Web sites related to the subject of this book. This site is updated regularly. Please use this link to access the list:
www.powerkidslinks.com/gdino/giganoto/